MW00773835

i

c

o

p

e

CCM Design by *Michael J Seidlinger*
Letter scribble by *Heiko Julien*
Cover background image by *Mesmeon*
http://mesmeon.tumblr.com/
ISBN - 978-1-937865-21-4

For more information, find CCM at:
http://copingmechanisms.net

I AM READY TO DIE A VIOLENT DEATH

Heiko
Julien

am i cool

27 May 2012

If I were to tell you a story about a Man, the discerning reader would put a stop to this right away and say, "No thanks, this seems like it's been done before."

And they would be right: This is true and it has.

If I were to tell you a story about several men and women, perhaps this would make for a more Engaging experience.

Perhaps not.

It really is nearly impossible to tell because there is no way of knowing precisely what is going on in your head.

Perhaps if I told you a story about myself.

Chapter 1

A small Asian girl swam faster than me at the pool today.

She was doing dolphin kicks and everything.

I got out of the pool to go to the bathroom and her brother took my lane and I wasn't even mad.

I think this is a good sign.

I think I am a Good person.

Chapter 2

I am the proud owner/inventor of the Dankest Spice Rack.

Possibly of all time.

Hydroponic rosemary, sage, cumin, thyme etc.

They're actually too potent.

Eating has become a dreadful chore.

LADIES—

Hi yes hello there.

I am the guy who makes your life complete.

With lovin' yes, but also tender sentiments that have deep, profound meaning custom tailored to your fine butt.

Before you came along, I was lost.

Now you are here and I still feel bad about myself, but I feel pretty good about you most of the time.

I like the way you look.

I like the way you make me feel.

I enjoy being in a relationship, haha.

Chapter 4

LADIES—

Hello yes hi. I am the guy whom sucks. I am the one who ruined your life. I am the boy who made you feel Emotional (bad). I am the man who wasn't ready to be a dad. These days, I identify primarily as an ex-boyfriend. That part doesn't bother me as much as the fact that I forgot a promise I made to myself: to Live Every Moment Like It Was My Last (Because it might be).

I spent 17 minutes reading YouTube comments on a video of a guy with Bad Opinions (ugh) while shaking my head in disgust (wow).

I started an alias Gmail account and sent messages to all my old friends telling them what I really think is wrong with them. What is wrong with me.

Jeez, I am overwhelmed with Feelings.

This is the bad part of my life.

Chapter 5

Many dads have been living well out of spite for longer than they can remember.

I say soak up the rays when you get the chance, on vacation or any other time you can get away from the office, haha.

Drive your red car on the beach. Drive your red car on the beach and into the ocean.

As the car fills up with water, just keep going.

Remember, you wanted it this way.

Automatic windows don't work in a submerged vehicle.

You will have longer than anticipated to do whatever you want.

You could think about whatever you want.

You could just sit still.

Chapter 6

I want an army of lovers who defend me and help me with my problems.

Comb my hair and keep my house clean and spread rumors about my enemies.

I want people to do the things I tell them to do.

Everyone does. That's what makes us so cool.

I wouldn't even bother with most people if I didn't believe this.

What would you do if a bear rose up on its hind legs at you?

Would you calmly accept your fate or would you sing to the bear?

Would you finally put your talent to the test in the ultimate setting?

This is it~

Chapter 7

Slap my body with pool noodles until I am bruised and puffy.

Lock me in the sauna, stick a broom handle in the door handle.

I become vapor.

Hurl jumbo shrimp at my smoldering corpse.

It doesn't matter cuz I'm dead.

You can just dump the whole bucket.

Chapter 8

I am ready to receive and give love.

I want to make a personal connection.

I want to stick my hand in the computer and touch your bodies.

I am ready to die.

I am ready to lay down on the ground and fuse with sidewalk.

I want the kids to walk on my melted husk on the way to school.

I am ready to be your boyfriend.

I am ready to provide Emotional support.

I am stealing your Energy.

I am Making Everything About Me Again.

Chapter 9

Religious revival in the Costco cold cuts aisle (?)

I'm screaming at the top of my lungs.

Want divine wisdom and joy and Great Deals.

My friend's mom used to speak in tongues at church but then she got self conscious about it and stopped.

I find this to be a minor tragedy.

Someone told me that Stevie Wonder wrote most of his songs doing glossolalia and added the words later.

I want to live my life this way, but most of the time it just doesn't seem like the right thing to do.

Chapter 10

I need to fall in love for selfish reasons. Got a big hole
I need to fill (*clumsy sexual metaphor, dELTE LATER.*)
The Taco Bell I was in on Saturday night had two se-
curity guards. I bought a taco and ate a taco on some-
one's 'beware of dog' porch. No dog.

My life means a lot to me.

Right now I am watching a tornado on the sun (online)
and I think I might cry.

Chapter 11

Quick heads up: The main character of the Great American Novel (unwritten) will be named 'Dude Online.'

Quick semantic healing exercise: I think your butt is great and I think you're going to make a great mother or father or sport coach one day.

Quick reminder that: I love you.

I love you so much it makes me sad and I don't remember why I loved you in the first place. This part isn't a semantic healing exercise. This part is the part where I forgot myself for a moment and I made a mistake. I don't think you can really love someone that you don't like and I don't really like you that much anymore so I probably shouldn't have said anything at all.

take me to the beach rub a medley of oils into my scalp get me ready for a long day of lounging

It freaks me out that my parents have known me since I was a child and don't have a problem with this. Do baby boomers feel mocked by the sensual and sexual overtones of mainstream classic rock, the withering score of their rapid decline into oblivion? It used to be in cooler commercials, for Hot Cars and Babe Beer. Now it's being used less coolly. Like, to punch up the notion of investing or saving your salary.

I don't need to wonder what it feels like to be old, I have always known.

I have always been old.

I have always been everything and I have always known that everything is happening at once—simultaneously—and I think I have never gotten enough credit for how gracefully I've handled this terrifying reality.

Chapter 14

Names white people will give to their children in the future or possibly in the present:

Brantler

Craydence

Bonard Consequence

Sit-down restaurant

Pleats von Buscular

Artisan Goodboy

"Dark" Mark

Tyrion Lannister

The McRib is Back

Barack Obama The Girl

Volitional Lotion

Chapter 15

As a little kid, I was reading a nature magazine about deer.

I remember feeling an aggressive impulse toward the fawn.

Even though I liked deer, I wanted to squish it.

And I felt very guilty about it.

And tried to talk about it but I don't think anyone knew what I was trying to say.

There's cognitive dissonance everywhere.

Everything is kind of like that I think.

A weird confluence of aggression and compassion.

Sex is basically that.

So is love.

So am I.

Chapter 16

"I Was In The Spirit World Thugging Heavily," the status read. An amusing notion, but probably not true.

Becoming increasingly disillusioned due to the fact that the kind of Disney feminism I was raised with seemingly has no practical applications in my actual life.

"I Am Not A Prize To Be Won."

Wow—no one cares because nobody wants a piece of this (me) (my butt) (:().

Need to re-evaluate my situation and make some more realistic goals.

Need to raise funds to build a sugar glider aviary.

Need to remember my Kickstarter password.

Considering becoming a life coach. Clients will be assessed rigorously. Engagement and awareness levels will be assessed by determining how likely they would be to try heroin if it was offered to them by offering them heroin.

Please note that I will not be coaching any losers through heroin addiction.

That isn't what I want to do with my life.

Chapter 18 - *autobiographical chapter*
(painful and revealing)

True Story: My wife left me for a finely crafted grilled vegetable artisan sandwich.

Chapter 18 : *(alternate)*

i want to ball hard in different aspect ratios

Chapter 19

You meet people and they are mirrors of yourself.

You give them the love you want in return, and you feel happy in this moment.

Chapter 20

I fell asleep on the street cuz I was pooped and several dogs wandered over to me and took a nap too because they trusted me.

I am probably going to have very beautiful daughters and average looking sons.

Chapter 21

Is it ethical to dream to be a Man of the People who is slightly better than The People?

Here is one weird tip the government and the cops do *not* want you to know.

You can control your feelings with your thoughts.

Chapter 22

Spent a lot of time with my grandma today.

She showed me pictures of her family from the 1940s.

They lived on a farm in Southern Illinois.

Now I'm thinking about death.

As a child, the notion that sex is a primitive act occurred to me while watching an episode of *Home Improvement*.

I still feel this way, I think.

I'm not sure if it's doing me any good.

Chapter 23

A man wants to have sex. You cannot trust him for this reason.

Even if he has a trill aura~

I bet cave people used to just go wild with sex on each other but I'm not sure if this was the right thing to do or not.

If you were capable of feeling all the love of all the people who had ever been in love before, you would probably cry.

If you were capable of feeling all the pain and sadness of all the people who had ever fallen out of love before, you would probably cry.

I think people are always crying for different reasons.

I am crying for different reasons.

Chapter 24

I went to a *Blink 192* concert when I was 12.

The only reason I was born is because my dad asked my mom to borrow a guitar pick at the mall once long ago. My mom kissed Barack Obama in the 70s. My dad had a brief affair w/ Madeline Albright in the early 80s.

I wonder if they ever discuss this.

There exists a VHS tape of me as a child w/ Rat Tail Hairstyle, somewhere. Fast forward to the year 2012 and I am lifting weights in my bedroom, repeating to myself, "This is making you happy."

I'm getting swole.

Sometimes people want to hang out with me and all I want to do is sit in a bathtub, eat yogurt, and read the Bible cuz I'm wise.

Is it possible to sympathize with a Fat person on vacation?

What if they dropped their ice cream cone on the boardwalk and looked up at you in a glum fashion?

Chapter 26

Because I am a tolerant and compassionate and Good person, I always try to see things from others perspectives. For instance, my dad is a jerk.

The moral of this chapter:

No Gods. No masters. No dads.

Chapter 27

Posted an Instagram of my custom NPR tote to Pinterest.

A cop mocked me in the comment section.

RIP Dream Of The Progressive Bourgeoisie.

(me)

I have spent time flexing my muscles in my life.

I have spent Emotional time with a girl.

I have renounced reality before.

But reality didn't care.

So I accepted it again.

everyone deserves to be naked and flying

Special Announcement/Disclaimer (Not a Chapter)

If you confuse reality with your perception of reality—
wow—you are really screwed up and I don't want to
know you.

Chapter 29

If I had to choose one word to describe my spirit's essence it would be 'shorts.'

Did You Know? Local teens are at risk to take performance-enhancing drugs so they can do better at Chatting Online.

Local parents need to be aware of these things.

Talk to your children. What else is there to do as a person but talk to other people?

If you don't like other people then you are probably not a very good person, or at least not very good at being a person.

To be a person is to love other people and to hate other people.

It is to accept negativity while accentuating positivity and not ignore either (not easy!).

I don't think anyone is all that stupid or dumb.

I think life is hard. I think anyone who is still alive is tough and strong and deserves your respect for this reason.

If not for this reason, then the fact that you have very little actual idea what it really feels like to be them any given moment should be enough to at least be curious.

And then you could ask them. And then you could make a friend.

That's all there really is to do.

I Am Ready to Die a Violent Death

15 Aug 2013

You know how dogs aren't really smiling, they're just panting? And they don't really kiss you, they just lick your face because they like salt? A lot of things are like that. I am like that.

People like dogs because they usually look happy. You can do this too. Dogs aren't always happy and neither are you.

There are a lot of things I really really want so I am smiling. I am smiling like I don't want to die alone.

We are smiling at each other like we don't want to die alone. This is probably the right thing to do.

Chapter 1

My zen so fresh don't never catch me not being real no no.

Our ideal western courtship begins:

See me inventing new yoga moves in the McDonald's Playplace.
Ask me out to dinner at a different McDonald's.
Save the date for our Fast Food Wedding.
Preacher wears the drive-thru headset.
Ring bearer rolls up to the second window and delivers the ring.
Bride and groom's families in the main dining area.
Kids in the ball pit.

Chapter 2

I want straight up bliss.

Want you to pour warm water down the back of my shirt while I'm at work and I'll pretend to get mad and then we go home.

Push me off a cliff, and here's the twist: The inside of the canyon is full of the stuff dreams are made of. Talking every *Nirvana* CD down here.

Human beings will be back in the forests sooner than we think, ripping bark off of trees and crushing skulls on rocks. It's a comforting thought.

Stick with me and I'll show you everything I know about how to make cool jpgs on the computer and also true love.

I will take care of you even though I don't believe in that sort of thing.

The Native Americans used to use every part of the buffalo.
Including the pink slime.
Just wander out into a cornfield and eat some corn.
This is America.
This is God's country.

Chapter 3

Pitching a TV pilot where I teach kids how to live cool lives by learning to enjoy common things like putting their shoes on slowly and drinking water in real-time.

Like to think I could pull off a certain post-9/11 Mr. Rogers vibe. Fancy myself an otaku *Captain Kangaroo*. Steampunk Mr. Wizard and all I want from you is actual friendship.

But I'm still.
Real Life Bart Simpson.
Yeah I'm throwing cats into a basketball hoop by their tails.
Haha. pizza for breakfast.
Turtle power.

I'll never die.

Here is an interesting scenario: You are trapped on an elevator with the guy who did the voice of the cat from *Sabrina the Teenage Witch* (Nick Bakay) and he wants to talk about race.

Just stay cool. We just stay cool together.

And we are dancing.
Like we know people.
Out There.
Want to take our money.
And kill us.
And we still think they are beautiful.

Hot Tip: Everything in life can be quantified positively or negatively.

Your friend says hello to you:

+5 pts

Your mom thinks you are mad at her:

-10 pts

You watch an episode of *Frasier* on Netflix with your brother and identify with the main characters because they are also brothers:

+10 pts

You don't have a very close relationship with your adult siblings:

-15 pts

You know your dad doesn't like your music very much:

-15 pts

He pretends that it is all right but just not for him:

+5 pts

Sometimes I feel like everything I'm doing and saying is a rude parody of the truth and my reward for this witty satire is being sad.

when your computer dies, you're supposed to eat it

Chapter 7

I am afraid of men but I am a smart boy so I intellectualize my fear in the form of Cool Shaming and Tight Blaming.

If I'm being honest, I would like to be the Number One Dude. I admire strong guys. I like to watch them play sports. I relate to the idea of a Buff Bro. I like a dude so top heavy I can topple him with a good push. I like to push dudes into pools in the summertime.

But I guess what I most want is to be in actual love with a woman who actually loves me back until we die painless, unexpected deaths simultaneously, but someone told me this was already done in a Bad Movie.

Regardless, I should probably try to be less of a Fucker and more of a Lover if this is what I really want out of life.

It's hard when you're designed to fuck. And kill. And tear raw flesh to shreds with your sharp pointy teeth.

2/5 fucker 3/5 lover is the optimal formula for a Good Man, I think, but I'm addicted to being an idiot and it's a problem.

But I like you. I want to go to the mall with you just to walk around.
And I love you now.
I love you like a rabbit loves the fear.

Chapter 8

Imagine if on warm summer nights in the suburbs, the neighborhood dads all hung out on the corners and roughhoused and didn't want to go home.

Incidentally, I can trace the root cause of my disillusionment with the human condition to finding out that all hair is dead.

Quick role-playing exercise: A tall man wants to be nice to you. What do you do?

(You are a beautiful female dog.)

Less incidentally, it is Monday and I am wearing a teal t-shirt. I am hiding in a potted plant at the food court.

What if you did something really sexy and the only one who saw was your dog?

Would you have to get married? Probably not but its fun to think about.

You can see a lot of Rare Vids of Young Dudes hanging out at home and doing funny voices if you search 'Just Chillin' on YouTube.

Go ahead and try this and maybe then you will learn how to love without needing to receive anything in return.

Chapter 9

Wow dude, I think you have the Most Pretentious Dad.

He just said "In vino veritas" in a British accent and took a big swig of Gatorade.

One time I went to see *X-Men First Class* with my brother and did deep breathing exercises throughout the entire film.

When it was over, was like, "Wow, that was a good movie."

Chapter 10

Tailgate at my funeral.

Just make a straight up mockery of my sweet and gentle legacy with grilled meats and vulgar cursing.

I want to be a hard working man.

I want to make bad decisions in a forest while my creature friends take notes.

Push me off the empire state building into your open arms.

Wrap me in swaddling cloth and drop me from a helicopter into the ocean.

Toss a jalapeno popper into my gaping body.

Need some spice in my life.

A timeless boyfriend will love you forever.

A thyme-less boyfriend lacks spice and has poor 'thyming' in bed.

Haha.

Chapter 11

Imagine an orgy large enough to render government obsolete. Now make your dreams a reality. You have a Facebook, probably.

Don't say it isn't possible.

I cannot believe that people still watch television so I am going to pretend that they don't. This is how it starts, denying reality. This is how people go insane.

If you just dive in maybe you can maybe just love it a lot, maybe.

A quick confession: My dad invented the genre of radio commercial where a kid wins a spelling bee by spelling quality with letters that make up the name of a business and I'm sad about it.

But in spite of hardship, I've had my fair share of innocent thoughts in my life. Here's one right now: Being warm can be fun sometimes but other times not so much.

Ultimately the most important part of your life is being old because that's the last part.

I believe this but I'm not sure if I'm looking forward to it or not.

Chapter 12

Culture began and ended when the butch kid from *Home Improvement* had that bowl cut ponytail hairstyle for a while. It began when he got the haircut and ended when he cut it.

Imagine if you had grown up on TV. Things would have been different for you.

Think fast hot shot. You *are* on TV and the camera man is a *bug*, and, think even faster, so are *you*. It is the year 2020 and the government (one-world) has made love illegal.

Now what do you do?

Stay cool.

I can imagine in a certain sense it would be really exciting and interesting to be attacked by a shark in open water, but this is only because I've seen it on TV.

So now you maybe are starting to get a sense of how serious all of this actually is.

Chapter 13

Would you wear a t-shirt that read I Am Watching TV
And I Feel Like Shit?
How about I Stared Into The Void And All I Got Was
This Lousy Ennui?
How about I Checked My Privilege, Now I'm Dead?
How about The Meek Shall Inherit The Girth?

You are staring at me with your arms folded and I am
starting to think you are not the kind of person who
would even wear a t-shirt and now I don't even know
who you are anymore.

Chapter 14

Need enthusiastic college freshman who cares to shame me for living in a house. Via email or text. Will pay you in the coolest kind of cigs. I don't deserve to be shamed, I just enjoy it. I am very well behaved. Eat three bowls of oatmeal per day because I just like the texture. I am just getting by.

I am a very technological boy. Programmed my mom's boyfriend's mobile phone to send me Date Updates with regularity. They're at Red Lobster? OK.

I am very mad about a television show and am spending hours trying to find the combination to my step-dads gun lock.

66642069 911666420▲ 69▲69▲▲ 69696▲▲▲. Nothing is working.

Now I am an older boy and I am getting a half sleeve tat of my own mouth saying, 'Do Patriotism Not Irony' because I think it is stupid and so am I.

Now I am an ever older man and I am getting to that age where my favorite thing to do is just spend time. I don't want to spend all my time with you, but I need to. I need someone to be accountable to or I will spend all day on the Internet telling other people their opinions are wrong.

I need you to french me into the fucking dirt. Need you to actually care about me and I need you to know that I just get tired sometimes. Need to think that you are a better person than I am and never say it. Need you here with me, on our actual deathbed, laying perfectly still in the middle of every single consecutive and increasingly sober night.

That's all I need because I know no one ever really says what they really mean and I know that there exists a world beneath this one where all the things that get left unsaid become all the things you really want. It's my mom's basement, but I can't go back.

It's just you and me, girl. Let's wilt into this sleep number and feed off the energy of commercials. Let's get really into shows. Let's get better at eating food. Let's just go through it all together and never stop going through it.

I love you like a rabbit loves the fear. Said this before, but it bears repeating.

I love you like a rabbit loves the fear~
I love you like a rabbit loves the fear~
I love you~

since chapter 3, i have gained 700 pounds. there is no going back

Chapter 16

Rapping was accidentally invented in 19th century Russia when a baker coincidentally rhymed a bunch of orders during peak business hours.

I'm in the very bottom of the trashcan and people keep gently tossing banana peels onto my face and body. As far as I know this is legal.

I think people are prone to suicide because we can experience so much joy. It's a risk reward thing and it's treacherous as shit but very profitable. I like to think of my life as a business and I am the CEO. Haha. I think I am making a lot of 'money' all the time.

Sometimes think I deserve to be treated like Shit by a Beautiful Woman. I'm jogging 4-5 times a week now, getting fit for this crucial life experience.

Incidentally, there actually are full sized alligators in the sewers of New York City and I know because I had sex with one of them.

Chapter 17

Load me into the barrel of a gun and fire my ass into international waters.
I want to do things only fish would tolerate or even understand.

And sometimes I am engulfed with passion. In the heat of the moment, I got confused and excited and ruined my own life.

I kissed a dog on the mouth where its lips could be.

Destroy me.
Love me.
Warp my image in Photoshop with filter presets.

Push me off the brink of sanity.

Edit my *Sister, Sister* fan fiction without my permish.

Chapter 18

This chapter is called 'I Went To College.'

If a burglar broke into your house and said, "Where is all your anime I'm going to steal it," you'd have to tell him, according to Kant.

Lol. No, dude.

A pun: Jane 'Air' (Eyre) Bud. Haha.

Nietzsche wouldn't approve of *Looney Tunes*. Übermensch shaming. Get it Wile E.

(That's all I learned.)

if a meteor can take the dinosaurs away it can bring them back

Chapter 20

And I have always known that nothing really matters and all of a sudden I love it so much. Because I have stared into the void and it has given me strength.

I know there is nothing, and it makes me strong.
I know I am nothing, and this is a major load off my mind.
I know I am everything, and this is what I really want.

Heiko Julien

I realized I know the truth.

More than I was allowing myself to engage with.

I know that this is it.

And that I am going to die.

But I also know that I do things that I love.

And that I know society is bullshit.

And that this will all be over.

And there will be no me to remember any of it.

And the only reason to do anything is for love.

As a means to love.

So that's what I am going to do.

I need to be me.

I've always known who I am and was afraid to be that person.

But I'm that person now.

And I'm never going to stop.

Ricki Lake

You are gaining that energy we talked about.

You are drawing energy from the void.

Heiko Julien

!!!!!!!!!

When I Am a Dog I Am Barking

1 Mar 2013

I killed myself in 2007.

My parents made all my aunts, uncles, and cousins take time off work to come to the funeral. Some of them had to fly in from out of town.

I woke up as a golden retriever in my neighbor's backyard and missed the whole thing so I'm not sure how it went or if anyone cried.

My new family did not get an invitation.

My master is a stay-at-home-dad named Tom who is usually in a bad mood.

He has a riding lawnmower and stands underneath my parents' window coughing at night, sometimes for hours.

He mows his lawn three times a week.

He's a weird guy. He named me Bob.

It has been six years and I am an older dog now.

I have learned a lot about myself.

The grass is nice on my feet in the summer when the sun shines but sometimes I still just want to be let back inside.

I like it when I am running and there are lots of things to smell.

I have two boys I play with. They are Tom's sons.

They like to play basketball in front of the house.

They lower the hoop so they can do slam-dunks and I watch them from the window in the living room.

When the boys were little, they used to like to pretend with toy swords in the backyard. They were slower then but they had more energy.

Now one of them has a real sword. He swings it around in the backyard and makes noises while his brother and I watch.

Sometimes he chases me. I'm too fast and he can't catch me with the sword.

My old family doesn't go outside that often. I am actually not sure if they live next door to us anymore or not.

There is still pain. I can see fewer colors than I could before.

I do not understand why a lot of things are happening and sometimes it bothers me.

When I'm confused I get frightened and bark.

When I am barking, Tom yells at me to stop. If I don't stop, I get put outside.

I get upset. It passes. I wait to be let in.

Sometimes I'm a 'good dog'. Sometimes I'm a 'bad dog.'

I don't really get it. I don't understand how these things work.

I am a bad dog.

I want things very badly at certain moments.

I want things so badly I react with all the energy I have without reserve.

I feel like I am almost constantly reacting or desiring something I cannot have.

I need a lot of things. I struggle through a fast haze. I lust in a dull blur.

It's draining and sometimes I just want to be told what to do.

There have been at least two movies made about people who have died and then became dogs, at least that I was aware of when I watched movies.

In both of these stories, the protagonist-turned-dog tries to go back and fix their old human life.

I am not that kind of dog.

I think that if you are trying to fix your past human life

when you are a dog, you must not be doing a very good job of being a dog at all.

I think that I like it when I am running.

There aren't as many colors to see but lots more things to smell.

Sex
Is Real
and It
Affects
the Future

31 Mar 2013

I'm sitting in my car in the parking lot of a Walgreens across from a Burger King, opening a package of Ny-Quil and this bottle of cough syrup I just bought.

If I were a Burger King, I would be closed right now.

If was a Walgreens, I might still be open because some Walgreens are open 24-hours a day. If you were a Walgreens, you would be the kind that sold alcohol.

If you were a Burger King, you would also be the kind that sold alcohol. You would be one-of-a-kind.

You would be the only one that does what you do.

It's cold today, like yesterday and probably tomorrow too. My car is freezing and I'm sitting here rubbing my hands together and coughing up green mucus and thinking about earlier today when we talked on gchat.

I told you I hadn't seen Brian lately.

"i was going to this weekend but i got sick," I said.

"he's so married anyway."

"so married lol," you said.

"guy works like 90 hours a week. like 90 high school english teacher hours a week," I said.

"hard life," you said.

"so all his free time is married time," I said.

"when are we getting married ;~)" you said.

"yeah its terrible it sounds absolutely awful the more i saw of what that job is actually like the more i was like uhhhhh," I said.

"lol we arent getting married," you said at 7:53 PM.

"yeah i guess i dont see you with that kind of life," you said at 7:55 PM.

"you dont love the kids enough," you said.

"you have to give your life up to them."

"i dont love everyone. i dont have a savior complex and i dont want to Save The World," I said.

"you sure dont" and "ha," you said.

I told you I meant it and you said you knew.

I said I thought most people didn't want to save the world and you agreed.

I told you that you didn't either and you said that was true too.

But you told me I had changed a lot, that when we met I was 'super zen zen free world' and now I wasn't.

"i was going thru a phase I guess."

You said I am always going through phases.

You said I am constantly changing and that it was fine if that's how I needed to be but that it was hard for you.

You said you would probably never really know me.

I am sitting in my car in the Walgreens parking lot

across from the Burger King and I don't have anything to chase my NyQuil with so I am being efficient by taking swigs of cough syrup with each pill. I am guessing I have a fever of 101-102 degrees so I will probably need three NyQuil.

Cough syrup tastes like something you shouldn't be putting in your body. This is what I think as cough syrup enters my body. It feels like a feat of strength to force all three of these big green gel-disk pills down with the synthetic red-flavored goo. Swallowing them is equally unpleasant but I feel a sense of accomplishment having stomached the last pill. This good feeling abruptly turns to something along the lines of fear and shame as I realize I have accidentally drunk three-quarters of the bottle on accident.

I've known people who have drank cough syrup recreationally. They seemed shitty. I feel pretty shitty right now. This is the reasoning I use to justify drinking the rest of the bottle. I am going to get shitty, I guess. This will be a heinous adventure, maybe. 'When in the shit, get shitty,' I suppose.

Syrup coats my throat as I start driving with a sense of urgency, heading instinctively in the direction of the mall. The mall is warm. You can sit still in the mall. There are people at the mall.

As I drive, I make an effort to recall what I know about the psychoactive effects of over-the-counter cough medicine. It's a *dissociative*, I remember. People who drink it walk around like robots because they feel separate from their body. I saw a guy do this at a party once. He looked weird and shitty to me, but he seemed ok with it.

Dissociating from your body and mind could be an invaluable experience, especially today. I am ready to go outside of myself right now. I didn't want to be here anyway.

It takes about 35 minutes to get to the mall. I pull into the parking lot outside of Sears upon arrival. My stomach does not feel good. Starting to feel like I am pregnant with poison and my newborn child will be a terrible nightmare baby. Cough syrup anti-Christ child of shit. Feel like my baby will be born violently into this world out of my own ass in the Sears bathroom in t-minus 5 minutes or so. I also notice that my cough is gone and I try to be grateful for this for a minute but my stomach wont let me. Time to get moving.

I move to exit my car and am immediately struck by an intense gravitational sensation. As I stand up, I feel like I left every part of myself but my rotted stomach in the front seat. I am a floating brain and little cartoon bubbles may or may not be popping around my head right now.

There is no time.

I leave myself in the front seat and hustle like a goblin toward the pearly department store gates.

"I am so demon right now," I think.

My body reacts by laughing, which is even more surprising. Definitely very demon right now. Better keep it together, floating demon, I think, nearing the entrance.

These people will eat you.

The pronounced *woosh* of sliding doors announces

my arrival at Sears. Frigid breeze meets stale air-conditioned warmth as I march forward with purpose.

An old lady on a motorized scooter stares at me as I make my way down the aisle. We exchange glances that last a tiny eternity and I feel reassured as I enter the restroom.

The bright fluorescent light bathes me. I am relieved. I am born anew.

I am America's sweetheart.

I am a pure being of light.

I am an American Bad Ass.

I am Kid Rock's stepdad.

I emerge into my new surroundings, refreshed and uninhibited. Everything is buzzing a little. A soft hum colors things a bit. It colors them orange, I will say, because I want to and I can. I go with the orange flow of the department store stream, moving through the designated pathways until I am released into the open waters of the adjacent mall.

I have made it back to my natural spawning ground using only my intuition, I think, making what I imagine to be salmon noises by sucking in my cheeks and smacking my lips. People can see me doing this. Nothing a salmon like me ought to be concerned with.

I swim on through the wide-open brightness in the direction of the food court, also by intuition I suppose. The intensity of the light, the reverberation of sound against the floor and walls strikes me and it feels intense. I open my eyes wider and perk up my ears to take in more of it and shudder.

Too much.

An unexpected wave of excitement rises in me abruptly and it shatters my nerves for a bit, sending a stiff tingle up my spine. The sensation has a deep hold on me but I must voyage on.

No one else is going to colonize the prairie that is this mall.

I do not have dysentery yet and my wagon train of one is operating with four new wheels and four solid axles.

It is time to move. Adventurers cannot be afraid.

Walking toward me is what appears to be a family—a mother with three children. The mother is carrying one of her children, a young girl, in her arms. She is visibly struggling, sweaty and agitated. With her is what appears to be her son, having difficulty carrying another young girl. The girl doesn't appear to be much younger than he is.

"She's heavy," he says.

"Then you need to learn to carry her better!" she says back.

I can't process this. After a moment's reflection, I decide it is probably best not to. Mother and son shuffle past me carrying the girls while I walk past them robotically with my eyes unnaturally wide open, just trying to remain calm.

Right now I feel like I need something, but I am not sure

what. Everywhere I look around me, there are things. Things I could have. I could put these things on, in, and around my body. These things could make me happy.

I decide that I want a thing, but I don't know what I want and it makes me feel bad. It feels alienating to not know what you want, like a bad kind of dissociation, maybe. A midi version of the song, "Paint with All the Colors of the Wind," from *Pocahontas* plays in my mind and I just shake my head because it seems uncalled for.

People come here to get stuff. That is basically the whole point of a mall. My instinct brought me to the place where all the stuff is, didn't it? I should probably get some.

I make up my mind to get some stuff, but it feels sort of like giving up. Shouldn't there be something else? What kind of adventure is it to just go to the mall and buy something? The risk, intrigue, and romance I desire seem mocked by the Pocahontas song that pops back into my head.

Then I see it. The mall fountain. It is embarrassingly beautiful.

I approach it cautiously, careful not to get my hopes up in case it turns out to be some sort of mirage. I sit on its edge and carefully dip a finger in. I feel the water and it's so wet. I briefly survey the scene, then dunk my whole hand in.

Definitely wet.

Cool liquid shares vaguely familiar skin and I stop thinking about myself for a minute. The moment is fleeting.

I begin to feel somewhat creepy, imagining a nice family watching as a man gets sensual in some public water. I imagine the girl-carrying family watching me. The mom is not pleased. She covers her son's eyes with one hand while holding her daughter with the other. The son covers the eyes of the girl his mother is holding with his free hand, struggling to hold onto the girl he's holding with the other. The girl he's holding has no one to cover her eyes, so she just watches me feel the fountain. I'm not sure how she feels about it.

I dry my hand on my pants and thinking this is probably as good as I can do right now when the sensation of longing returns. I can't pinpoint where it is coming from exactly, but it is persistent and unpleasant.

I sit up to leave for the food court but feel conflicted. Shouldn't the fountain be enough?

No sooner than I find my shrine, I abandon it in search of a burrito or something. I'm not even hungry, my stomach is still tender from poisoning. On some level I know that I don't need anything. It feels like déjà vu and I make an effort to ignore it.

While I'm taking the escalator down into the food court, I watch the fountain splash water upward. I can see it behind a cell phone cover kiosk, the water in motion. Less and less of it is visible until it is gone from sight and I have been plopped down at the foot of the moving stairs.

I try to purchase a burrito without saying anything but fail when I have to tell the person in charge of the burritos that I want one. She hands me a bag of food and tells me to have a nice day. I wander off toward an arrangement of tables and chairs wondering if I have received the love I need when I see something else.

There is a carousel in the middle of the food court. Children wait in line to ride with their parents by their side. The carousel seats are all shaped like animals. There's a panda and a lion. There's a giraffe.

I wouldn't mind sitting inside a giraffe, I think, crinkling the bag of food with a dull hand.

I find a table close to the carousel so I can watch. The machine isn't operating quite yet. The kids are scurrying around, picking out which animal they want to sit in. I am rooting for the giraffe. Whichever kid sits in the giraffe has the right idea. Everyone gets settled and the ride begins. Unsettling music plays as the contraption slowly begins to revolve.

No one chose the giraffe.

I sit and watch the ride go round. When it's over, the kids get off and a new batch populates the plastic animals inside. The music starts up, the gears in the machine whir, and the whole process begins once more.

Again, no one has chosen the giraffe.

Seems pretty messed up to me but I try to accept it. I don't know what goes on in others people's heads sometimes or ever. From where I sit, in a mall food court with a neglected burrito lying in front of me getting staler by the minute, it seems as if you can never really know what is going on in another person's head.

I am thinking about what you said to me earlier on gchat.

You said that you would probably never know me.

It's probably true. You probably won't.

But isn't that how it has to be? How else could it possibly work when everything is constantly changing?

A few minutes ago, I bought a fresh burrito. Now my burrito is getting cold. The ingredients inside are congealing as I sit here thinking about them, getting mucusy and gross. The tortilla wrap is hardening into a shell. There is a time limit on this burrito I will miss my burrito-window because I'm not ready for it. I don't need it. I bought something I didn't need because I felt weird and couldn't stand my own thoughts, and now it is going to waste. This burrito and I are like ships in the night, or something, I think.

I wonder what that phrase actually means while I watch the carousel spin for a third time. My warped vision is pulsing, vibrating, the reduced frame rate jumping like a buffering video, and in this moment it seems clear to me that everything is always changing even though we don't want it to because that's what happens to things that move.

Everything is always changing, I repeat to myself.

I guess I am too. So are you.

A panda passes by with a happy toddler and his mom in it. I feel empty. This uneaten burrito seems like a tragedy happening in slow motion right in front of me and I turn away because I just can't bear to watch any longer.

Sitting at the table next to me are a group of teenage boys and girls, talking at each other and eating fries. I overhear some of their conversation.

"What I want to know is who changed my Facebook status to 'I'm gay,'" a boy says.

"It was up there for like a year because I don't go on there that often." His friends laugh.

"Do you guys know this guy who Dave is?" he asks. They don't.

"He recently came out of the closet and posted this long rant about how the pope said something against gay marriage and the only comment was 'You go, Glen Coco!'" They laugh, but less than last time.

As I get up to leave, I hear the boy call my name. He says he recognizes me. I recognize him too. He asks me if I had been a student teacher at his school and I tell him no, I hadn't.

He says he's pretty sure he's seen me. I tell him I'm not sure how that could be because I've never been a teacher, but I'm lying. I had taught at his school. I recognized him from class. As I turn to leave an empty giraffe passes and I stop short.

"Can I ask you guys a question?" I ask.

They say yes.

"If I was a teacher, I mean, I'm not, but if I was…"

A passing lion catches my attention, distracting me. It has a mother and two children inside it.

"Do I seem like I'd be an OK teacher to you? Like, do I look like I could stand in front of a class and teach it?"

They look at each other and don't seem to know what to say.

"Do I seem OK to you?"

The girls start giggling. The boy whose Facebook status had been changed for a year finally spoke.

"To be honest, you seem kind of fucked up to me, man. I mean, I'm sorry, but yeah."

The girls laugh and he grins at them.

"Sorry man, I dunno," he says and starts laughing too.

I sigh and look off at the carousel. It has stopped and everyone is getting off. I turn back to them and stare at the boy's face and eyes. He stops laughing and stares back at me. I feel like I want to say something important to him but don't know what I should say.

"Sex is real and it affects the future," I say with authority before returning to the fountain, taking my burrito with me.

Back at the fountain, I am in church.

I am in the front pew humming along, pretending I know the words.

I am at my family's ancestral shrine and am thinking about what it must have been like to live in the past.

I am a new born baby deer watching the shimmering light the fountain reflects through the backs of my placenta sealed eyelids.

But I still feel like I need something. I take out my

phone to text you.

"hi bb," I send to you.

A couple is sitting on the edge of the fountain across from me. The woman has a lot of shopping bags. She is on her phone and her boyfriend isn't.

"i want to carry you around like this family I saw at the mall today," I send to you.

"they were carrying their kids and i want to carry you through the mall forever."

My phone buzzes a few moments later.

"lol," you sent to me.

I take a picture of the fountain and send it to you.

You send me back a dolphin emoji with three shooting stars and a watermelon.

The couple across from me is not speaking. They are not watching the fountain either. The woman is looking at her phone. The man is looking at her shopping bags.

I wonder where you are supposed to find what you need.

I toss a quarter into the fountain. Nothing.

I toss my burrito into the fountain. Still nothing.

I jump in.

There Is No Reason for Tigers to Be Beautiful, They Just Are

31 Mar 2013

People have been honest with me. They've told me they want power.

Recently, I looked up the term 'intimacy' on Wikipedia and have been dealing with the repercussions ever since: A major sleep debt accumulated over several restless nights, what little sleep I've gotten interrupted by frequent night terrors.

Dreamed I designed the Golden Corral logo and was reasonably well off financially as a result.

Dreamed my brother maintains a blog where he posts Upskirt Pics he's taken of mannequins while wandering around the mall on his lunch break. He works at the Vans store.

Dreamed I was driving into the city to see my girlfriend and saw a billboard that just read Voluptuous Homeboy in 72 pt. black Tahoma font over a white background. The billboard was paid for by the government. Typical, if you ask me.

I see myself posted up outside a surprisingly nice McDonald's. I enter and there's a chandelier. They let me behind the counter for some reason. Thought, This cannot end well.

Now you are dreaming too. You are dreaming that you've krumped off the sears tower and into a fulfilling long-term relationship with a thoughtful / sensitive / sexually attractive Lover who understands you.

You are standing in a crowd of slack jawed onlookers watching me pistol-whip a Baked Alaska at the Policeman's Ball. Now everyone's chanting my name. Making friends and influencing people is easy when you're mad, but this is a lesson you will not learn until Lindsay Lohan's mom gives you a pants-down spanking in Urban Outfitters for 'mouthing off' and nobody does shit. There is no justice on this Earth, but I don't blame her. She's just a person, and so are you. Other people are like you but they aren't you. I am like you but you are not me. Seems simple enough, but it is important to get the big things out of the way first.

Regardless, I have decided to make the most of my delusions and fantasies. They exist for a reason, maybe. They serve a function, perhaps. Tonight I am pouring cosmos into my coach purse until it is soaking wet. I am becoming the girl of my own dreams.

Let's Examine Love:
In the Case of Needing Someone But Not Liking Them.

The baddest bad boy in the history of Poor Decision Making is doing donuts on your lawn, but here's the catch: You are in love with yourself.

Touch my neck in the forest preserve near my parent's house. All trails lead back to the same place. This is a Safe Zone. Not a real forest.

Relate to me through popular song lyrics. Rub my back through this Eddie Bauer windbreaker in a Deep Thicket. Girl, we are truly Roughing it.

An underground VHS tape I purchased online called Greatest Underground Husband Tantrums 8 just arrived in the male. These hubbies are pissed and moaning. It's not that funny, but I'm just doing some research for the future. Want to know how to whine my way out of a tough jam.

This hubber is insanely jealous of his Sexually Attractive Wife. Pounding his fists into a bunt cake he made to prove he can Feminine Bake but is Masculine Strong. Seems like a cogent strategy.

This evening, I retire to my boudoir to relentlessly 'hump' a memory foam mattress just to prove a point: The point being that I am more on top of my game than ever before. A debatable claim, I'm sure, hence the urgency.

But what do you do once you have attracted a woman? Like, do you have to keep talking to her?

Baby, I have something to tell you: I am cheating on you with Mrs. Claus. But I love you, girl. I have loved you from the very beginning. I knew because when we first met I was interested in hearing about your pets (haha).

You make me stand up straighter without noticing.

You make me want to wear nicer pants.

Some people want to have arguments about what Love means.

I do not.

I want to talk about how it feels.

I actually don't want to talk about that anymore either.

If I Got Really Intense on You, Would that Be a
Problem? I Want to Put an Idea in Your Head:
Breathing Isn't that Easy.

Reduce complex problems into false dichotomies to
comfort yourself in the face of paralyzing ambiguity.

Choose to focus on the negative side of your fraudu-
lent binary, further reducing the scope of reality's con-
sequences and increasing the depth of your superficial
comfort.

Congratulations, you have made yourself feel Good
by feeling Bad. Likewise, you have made yourself feel
Bad by making yourself feel Good.

I ask myself, if neurosis is an attempt to avoid real
pain, will accepting actual pain treat it? Should I hire
someone to whip me with a flyswatter? To be honest, it
is difficult to hold myself accountable to anyone or take
responsibility for my actions because I am so much
smarter than everyone else. Been winning arguments
at my local Gamestop all afternoon by proclaiming my-
self to be a Realist before making my point. This is too
easy.

I drive home with an unearned sense of satisfaction and
make a conscious effort to live up to everything Chillaxing
may entail. It's a lot of pressure, but the cool thing about
excessive comfort seeking is that if you do it well enough,
you get to be alone all the time. You can work on your Life's
Work. That's what I do. For instance, I am watching a na-
ture documentary and just feeling sorry for everything.

People accumulate damage, but growth is the only True Love. In all honesty, at any given moment, I would rather be experiencing Intense Pleasure. This reminds me of a musing I have yet to profit from. Kraft Macaroni and Cheese should change their slogan to 'Ladies Love It,' and they probably will after they read this.

The coolest people are the ones who remind you that they live in the best city. They are cool because they've been to all the cities and they know. Sometimes the people you need aren't where you are. This is possibly unfortunate. Sometimes people are worth more together. This is probably tragic. Either way, our fates are more or less sealed, but there is an ample amount of wiggle room to make it worthwhile/cool/tolerable.

I just want you to imagine Jerry Seinfeld researching for the movie *Bee Movie* by watching bee footage.

Now imagine yourself doing what you really want to do with your own life.

Your Life Is Like An Adam Sandler Movie Because In The End Everything Works Out Pretty Well for Adam Sandler

Even Though I Consider Myself to Be the Hero of My Own Life, I Was Honorably Discharged from the Military for Taking Too Many Baths and Singing and Bothering the Other Soldiers with My Sensitive Voice.

This afternoon I am sitting on a park bench. I am watching a man maintain balance on roller blades while chatting up a Major Babe and deftly controlling an excited pug.

Thinking, 'This guy will never commit suicide.'

Now I am thinking about my life. I wish it had gone differently. I had a three-year relationship with the girl from the Verizon Wireless commercials before she was on TV and I'll be honest, it hurts to watch her have so much success.

However, despite my failures, I am not so short on successes myself. Will Smith wants me to come to his backyard BBQ & Swim Party to lecture his kids on how to be better people, but I am teaching my mom about zen.

Michael Jordan invited me over to his house to watch YouTube videos on his projector but I am busy talking to my dad about mistakes he's made. Michael Jordan's wireless network is called HisBadMajesty23Man and the password is 'Pussy' (go figure).

But presently, in this blissful instant, I am high on caffeine, imagining petting a dog.

I will not waste this grace.

I will rise to meet the moment.

Going to write **Real Power / Real Results** in sharpie on my forearms and challenge the strongest lifter at the gym to an arm wrestling competition to prove to kids that it's ok to be a loser.

It is three hours later and I did not do that. I am, however, officially High On Life: Drank an expired milk chug (2%) and wrote an entire season of entourage episodes just because I liked the way it felt.

Now I am listening to "Lullaby" by Shawn Mullins and thinking about all the times I wanted someone else to stop talking so I could talk about myself.

Yeah, I'm sitting on my lily pad, feeling high-def.

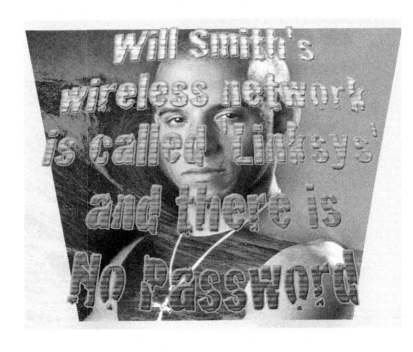

The Secret to My Decent Quality of Life?

I spend every moment I'm not eating thinking about the next time I will eat. Creates and maintains tension. This is how I have cultivated bliss within, and yet my greatest strengths are alternately my biggest weaknesses. For instance, I died in a house fire in 2004. Tried to make four toasts in a two-toast toaster.

You need to know: You are in the fight of your life. If you don't Grow, this fucked up hellscape of a reality we inhabit will ravage your mind/body/soul.

No pressure.

It is no wonder I've been a Bad Person and so have you. We'd like to think that's all in the past now. We are getting older and wiser and less terrified but the stimulus that scares us is getting stronger.

So let's talk about Bad People: Bad People betray their friends and themselves for no good reason because they have too much fear they've chosen to ignore rather than confront. On a seemingly related but unrelated note, this world has betrayed me, so I am commenting on YouTube vids, lamenting the death of Good Music. Forsaken by a culture that has abandoned me, I wander into my bathtub and drown. It was already filled from a previous bath. (Cold and gross.)

The fact remains that the majority of my youth is gone and I spent a lot of it being upset. Considering suicide as a means of avoiding future work and general discomfort, yet I look at you in your cargo shorts and think, 'You are not going to make it, probably.' I think this because I am a survivor and am also into men's fashion.

Animals are doing all kinds of crazy things to survive and so are you. You bought your daughter a Justin Bieber CD and listened to it to try to feel Good. Incidentally, I still cannot get over the fact that there are animals that live underwater.

You aren't allowed to commit suicide until your mom has died. These are the rules. I don't make them. Living is better than not living, even though it's painful a lot of the time. Just make plans for the future. You don't even have to do them.

When you are having a serious problem and there's no one you can talk to about it because they wouldn't understand, that's when you're you.

103

My grandfather was the first person to refer to a piece of fruit as being Gay. He said this during one of the wars when he forgot how to open an orange for a minute.

My grandmother was the first person to perform a downward facing dog in a Wal-Mart parking lot. Not sure why she did this. Lack the background knowledge to elaborate any further. (Sorry.)

Haters are always riding my jock, so if you want me to give you attitude, here it is: I got a big dick and I call my parents three times a week. I love my family, but I am getting to the age where when I tell people that I love my family, they assume I mean my wife and children. I don't. I mean my mom and dad. And my siblings, I guess. We've been through a lot together. When my brother was an Awkward Teen, my dad told him to call me for dinner. He said: "Dad wants you. Well, he doesn't *want you* want you." Then he walked away. I don't remember what happened next. (Sorry.)

My dad wears a hat all the time because he's bald and his head gets cold. This is the sort of integrity my generation is sorely lacking. I always interpreted Stay-at-Home Mom to be a command, but that seemed all right to me. Us kids grew up under a bridge so our mom was more of a Stay-Under-the-Bridge Mom. It is truly the hardest job there is. Most rewarding too. Bridges are really cool.

Seeing searchlights as a kid, I thought something really great was happening in some magical place in the distance. It was probably so wonderful they were lighting up the sky to let kids like me know where the cool things were happening. Maybe it was a Candy Factory Slumber Party, or perhaps that was where they filmed *Pokémon*. Found out when I was older that the searchlights were just coming from car dealerships, which is actually even better. Now I know where to find new cars.

Things get complicated for us Post-Kids, but the world has not passed us by. The solution is to be fashionable alone at night.

No one else needs to see this.

You can think your own private, beautiful thoughts, and forget them, wake up, and go to work.

Im the Best Looking Person In This McDonalds But The Fries Still Cost The Same

106

The Great Pun of the 21st Century Will Prove to Be Adding a B to Anal Sex in Order to Downplay All the Hype. History Will Bear Me Out.

It is strange to think that your parents are just other people. Becoming aware of this fact feels the way saying a word over and over until you realize it is just noise feels. I did this just now and am now wondering if music actually exists.

Coming to the conclusion that it does not because I have never actually seen it.

In the heat of the moment, I indignantly spit my Surge on the floor of this Alternative Rock Music Venue and skip out the door in 5/4 time. (I am making a statement about the predictability of pop music structures.)

Now I am back at home, slowing down YouTube clips of *The Price Is Right* audiences. I am watching celebrity funerals before I go to bed.

Now I am sleeping and I am dreaming again.

I am dreaming that my daughter is a Hot Server at a Pan-Asian Seafood Restaurant a lot of my close man friends attend regularly and it makes me uncomfortable. These men cannot be trusted.

People always reveal themselves to you. They want you to see what they want you to see, but this is not how it usually works.

People show their true selves to you when they least

expect it. Last week I saw an elderly gentleman's Fuck Face as he lifted a tire into the back of his van in the parking lot of an Ace Hardware.

Maybe the Name of the Game is to make the faces that you like, to feel the way your face likes to feel, but this is none of my concern at the moment.

I am overstaying my own welcome at my own celebrity-themed Halloween party, pop locking to the irregular beat of my own heart, dressed as myself (a famous author). Society has a lot of flaws, but I probably don't.

I am wearing a powder blue cardigan tied around my neck and I want to ravage you in the bushes of my family's beach house with (2) thoughts:

(1) Life is for Lovers
(2) People should have just never stopped being farmers

Just imagine how much progress we could make if people could be trusted well enough to communicate through a series of Rub Downs.

It's Probably Deep In The Jungle and It's Pretty Much Fine With That

Heads Up, Dipshit: A Bowl of Cheerios is Just Hard Bread Circles in Milk. That's Right, I'm Breaking Things Down One by One and Getting Major Results.

I am trying to become excited about my life again. Bought a football jersey with another person's name on it. I wear it around, but not the helmet. I'm not crazy.

You can trust me. I own several small animals including America's finest pet, the Dog.

I must admit, however, it does get lonely around the house. Last Sunday afternoon I was feeling Ready for some football so I swallowed a pigskin whole. I felt nothing. I said to myself, "I feel nothing."

Lately I have not been feeling things on a level that I once did.

I remember noticing the light change in a room as a boy and thinking I was the only one who noticed because everyone else ignored it.

I remember thinking I was the only person whose memory was stimulated by the smell of wet earth in the springtime.

Now, all these years later, I have forgotten how to fall in love with things, so I just go around trying out Funky New Eateries in my town.

This is my reward. I played by the rules and now I get to eat different kinds of meals outside of my house.

Everything happens for a reason, is what I always say. For example, I have spent my entire life eating various foods so I would know which ones I would want to keep eating later.

Measured decision-making has not always characterized my lifestyle, however. In fact, it was only last summer that I bought what I thought was a cigar from a gas station with a bulletproof glass window. It smelled like fruit so I gave it to my step dad when I got home.

He said to me, "Years of having white skin have made you hopelessly insane. Now take that pineapple blunt rap and go back to the gas station and work there."

So I did, and now I know the Value of a Dollar. (Just $1.)

Indeed, the working man's struggle is fraught with peril. Forgot the hyphen in Reasonable-Ass Man on my job application and now everyone at this Wendy's thinks I'm some sort of butt philosopher.

I want to be from a small tribe.

Want to dance with my childhood friends around a fire.

Want to grow my own food.

I want to die defending my wife in a field against people who hate us.

A human being needs humans to love and humans to hate and I am a human being.

Two people are having sex against the railing of the Grand Canyon.

It gives way and they fall in and don't stop till they hit the bottom.

That is the kind of life I want for us sometimes.

Other times I wish you wouldn't move past me so fast.

It is early in the morning and we are underneath the covers and underneath the covers is Antarctica and we have to huddle together for warmth.

I am wondering if you are ok even though there is no reason why you wouldn't be.

I am pressed against your warm body and feel concerned about our quality of death. I am worried about how you feel during your last sentient moments because someone told me your pineal gland releases a lot of DMT and you see a lot of things and feel a lot of things.

What if you felt guilty about your life?

Someone once wrote to me that they were "eating a hot dog with the same despair as a pilot who had fallen out of love with the sky," and that is how badly I need you right now.

My Grandpa on My Mother's Side Once Took Me Fishing at What I Would Describe As a Commercial Pond.

Like a network of little ponds stocked full of fish for people to just walk up to and stick their poles into. The fish are easy to catch because they don't have anywhere to go. They are probably bored and they would probably take any chance to get out of Fish Prison, even if they understood the implication of a lure.

We didn't just have a lure though. We used cheddar cheese that we bought from the grocery store as bait. My grandpa showed me how to put the cheese onto the end of the lure. I was young enough that I needed to be shown how to impale a soft thing on a hard thing, so I'm guessing I was pretty young. I don't remember how young, but I do remember the fish.

We caught a lot of fish that day. I felt satisfied and I decided I liked my grandpa a lot.

He used to call us The Family That Loves Each Other with a big smile on his face. I liked this, because he would usually call us this when my siblings, my mom, and I were all fighting. I think maybe we fought a lot, but I appreciated the support.

When I was a little older, my dad told me that he was not being supportive; he was just being a dick. They didn't really get along. My dad was in college while he and my mom were dating and my grandpa used to tell him that he (himself) Could Have Been A Lawyer if he had Wanted To. He told him this on more than one occasion.

My grandpa was not a lawyer; he was a cement truck driver. I'm not sure if he Wanted to be one or not. During the summer, when lots of construction was going on, my mother always used to point at the rolling cylinders mounted on the cabs of the cement trucks and tell me that Grandpa Used To Drive Those Cool Trucks.

She loved her father.

These are some of his Vital Statistics:

- ✓ He was short and bald.

- ✓ He drank a lot.

- ✓ He gambled away the family savings and would pass out on the front porch early in the morning after drinking all night.

- ✓ He got a 17-year-old girl pregnant and left my grandmother with 4 kids.

My grandmother knew about the 17-year-old girl. So did my mom. She and my grandpa decided to get married after they found out she was pregnant. I think you kind of had to in those days. Not sure if they wanted to or not.

Once at dinner, my mom asked them why their first child was born less than nine months after the wedding and my grandpa got very angry with her. My mom was young at the time, but she probably knew what she was doing. I don't think she bothered him about this again.

My grandpa avoided paying alimony to my grandmother. She never took him to court, but she did bother him about it pretty often, I would imagine. She had four kids, worked full-time, and wouldn't apply for welfare because she was too proud, I think.

One time, he agreed to give her some money and told her to send my mom's older brother to meet him at a bar where he was drinking with his friends. His friends were probably also construction workers.

Incidentally, I wonder if they ever did the thing where they Hooted & Hollered at attractive women when they walked past the construction site.

I wonder if they ate their lunches out of metal pails.

Ah, Tuna Fish Again, they might say.

Oh, There Goes An Attractive Lady, they might also say.

In my mind, they would say Lady because this is how I imagine grandpas talking in the past. Maybe I imagine this because I'm naive and/or dumb. Now that I think about it, they probably said something ruder because they weren't grandpas yet. They were just bros from the past and this would be consistent with the Hooting & Hollering.

Anyway, when my uncle met his father at the bar, he was given a bag of pennies and told something to the extent of Give This To That Bitch and all the people at the bar laughed. I wonder how this made my uncle feel. Maybe angry. Probably more sad.

He took the pennies home to her anyway. Pennies were worth more money in the past, but still not very much.

When my grandpa was older, he moved to the suburbs with the 17-year-old girl. She wasn't 17 anymore. By now she was somewhat of an old lady.

I don't know how old she was.

I do know she worked at Wal-Mart. One time, she complained at a family function that they made her clock out and keep working and said if she didn't, they would fire her. Seems like a pretty bad place to work.

This was after my grandpa had died.

While he was alive and in the suburbs, he had an above ground pool that I was really excited about swimming in. It had a chlorine dispenser designed to look like an alligator that floated around. I wasn't allowed to touch it.

My grandpa was very strict about his Pool Rules.

My grandpa died relatively young. He had a heart attack when he was 70 and he died. I think he had a stressful life.

I don't know if I am going to die young.

I might.

I wonder what will happen to me. I am certainly highly invested in the outcome.

I hope I get what I want, but there is no Reason why I should.

It is up to me.

There is no Reason for me to be here, I just am.

I decide why and it becomes real.

There is no reason for tigers to be beautiful, they just are.

There is no reason for you to be beautiful either, but you can be.

It's the thoughts that you think.

Be
the Girl
You Loved

10 June 2013

You can say things to me like, "You understand me," and I will smile and nod and the sound will work its way through me. I'll get the general idea and we may bond. We're alone together for a reason. You can tell me I am Perfect and I will smile and you may or may not stare into my iris and it might possibly start to look like the surface of another planet, or nebula even, if that's where it takes you. Or it might not. I won't know unless you tell me. Tell me so I can get the general idea and I can smile and nod and we can be there. We are here alone together for a reason, after all. Memories of love or lack of love travel through you at the sound of the word I just said, anchored by the heaviest gaze you can even sit with. The heavier we get the more we lie together, weighed down by words we've shared, tiny oral expressions passed ceaselessly back and forth for hours. This is how we've always tried to get out of ourselves and into each other.

I have used language precisely and in a way that communicated abstract thought before. Did it do me any good? I wouldn't feel remotely qualified to say.

"I would quit or join *the Beatles* for you."

Certain people are going to get you. They are going to take you, even. Take you away, and you're going to give yourself up. You're going to give yourself up willingly to them, these people who want you, because you are going to want to, more than mostly anything, I imagine. Maybe they will do things to you no one else has tried yet and even more people will happen. Maybe you will raise their children and maybe you'll resent them for it while your hot, young life fades fast.

What I'm saying is you could texturize me. I could fade you. We could spend all weekend together in my treehouse. We can blend together. I've melted before and had little to show for it. A person can get poured out after a while. I've seen it happen. It's as simple as being left up on a shelf or out on a table, someone just comes along and cleans you up after a bit. Can't blame someone for wanting to keep their space tidy and I'm not sure how else one ought to deal with goo. No, I don't want to melt anymore. What I'm looking for is a sort of mosaic experience. I want to be woven, is what I'm saying. It's a craft we can do around the house, master together in our own time, but once you're strapped in, you're hooked. You're attached.

I once saw feral cats mating when I lived on a farm in Hawaii. If you are not familiar with cat mating, that may be because domesticated cats usually go about it privately. Wild cats apparently don't, they did it right in front of us while their kittens watched in the backyard. An important thing to understand is that the male cat's member can be described like the spikes in a parking garage that come up to keep you from backing in. He enters and the prongs come out and there is no going back without consequence. I watched them with their kittens and the female's yowling rose from a low purr to a furious screech. He finished and she bit him and that was that. A violent act for sure, but what isn't? Have you gotten so far removed from what you are going through, what you are, that you don't realize in the very fiber of your being that all human interaction is political? Are you so shallow and lost that this seems tragic? If this makes you feel sad then you deserve it. It's the vibration of your goddamn soul collapsing in on itself and you need to fight it fiercely, a lot. Yes, I am certain that even when my mother was changing my lil' baby diapers it was political to a certain degree.

There are consequences for you and me. My neighbor told me, "I can't be the guy at the bottom of the stairs holding the flowers anymore." I can't either but I miss how awful it felt. The fact of the matter is I don't know who I was 7 years ago. That's the good thing about pain, you don't have to take it personally. It can create as intimate an experience as you want and you can build your own pyramids in you. Make your nervous system your ally, make your demons your slaves, and you can love me if you want. It's not my problem. Gandhi once told his wife he couldn't tell her that he loved her more than any other person because it wouldn't be fair. If you are intrigued and are wondering how you too can become this much of a baller, I will tell you how.

Be genuinely nice to people without expecting anything in return so they in turn assume your emotional energy is free and spend it freely. Love unconditionally until you get tired and stop. This is what is sometimes called a "long con," but if you are going to do anything well it is going to have to be done consistently over time. If you can convince a woman to marry you, imagine what else you could persuade her to do. Imagine what she will be able to convince you to do. Over time, both of your sexual orientations transform into the pained, anxious expressions on your faces when you aren't sure if you're going to get everything you want at a store. And you've chosen to feel bad about it. Will you perform unfathomable acts of cruelty to protect your dear, sweet ego? Wow, maybe.

But what if you weren't here?

What I'm saying is, you aren't and that's why it's so important to be here, now.

I will tell you I love you if that's what you want to hear. I will mean it if that's what you need. Don't take this the way it seems. We can have our love first and constructs second. You know that everything we do together is essentially an exchange of energy, right? People treat their energy differently. We have varying expectations of how much we think we deserve to receive and how much we are willing to give and what I'm saying is I want to figure it out with you.

Love Is Enough Except When It Isn't

16 Sept 2013

How you feel about something often has a lot to do with how you already felt.

Whatever it is, it's always lots of things at once.

We're on many different levels at once.

That's the only way this even works.

The wolf you feed wins and I've been a fractal this whole time.

I am infinitely dividing myself against myself.

The wolf you feed wins.

That's the only way this even works.

And summer is still happening.

Isn't that what you said you wanted.

All winter long.

How many reasons can you think of?

You know that when you're at the bank, that money is yours.

Right?

My friend texted me that the guy she's into told her he is going to keep her in bed for 3 days straight.

I hope he takes good care of her.

My mom texted me telling me that my dad was stung by a swarm of wasps this morning. I hope she takes good care of him.

Fear is a sickness and I have seen the Earth's only moon before with my own two eyes and didn't even care.

The passions of this dull planet run through me predictably and it is not a big deal.

I wear cutoff shorts all over my gentrifying neighborhood.

I told the barber to shave the sides of my head.

Some dude told me he has made love to many women who have my same haircut.

I hope he takes good care of them.

Love is enough except when it isn't.

My sister gets very irritated with me quickly.

When we were little, she used to sit me down and teach me lessons about how the world works. The other day I told her I think the President is a reptile and doesn't care about us.

She is disappointed. I was a bad student.

My sister met her boyfriend when he was working in the record shop she lived above. She left the bathwater running and flooded the ceiling of the store and he ran up to knock on her door to tell her to turn it off.

When they were first dating, he told her he didn't like sports that much, but that wasn't true. He likes sports a lot. He told me to download an app that will track how fast I can run around the block. They live together now.

I hope he takes good care of her.

This morning I went to the public swimming pool in my neighborhood. The teenage lifeguard girl told me I couldn't bring a bag out onto the deck. I had to leave it in the locker room, but I could take my things out of the bag and put them on the deck. It would be fine as long as I left the bag in the locker room.

She couldn't tell me why.

I hope one day we figure it out.

If Somebody Likes the Way Your Face Looks They're Going to Let You Get Away with a Lot More than They Would if They Didn't

But you are still against the law.

Trying not to feel self-conscious is the essence of self-consciousness.

And you're only a girl to me.

I'm always looking forward to the best new rappers.

When the Iraq war started, I thought they were going to show it on TV like football.

I'm always looking forward to the best new wars.

I think every one that's fought is better than the last because I'm an optimist.

You know they're just going to keep re-enacting the Civil War until they have another one.

When I take Adderall sometimes I get more tired than I would if I hadn't.

It's a thing we do, feeling like we need to put something outside of ourselves into ourselves to make us work.

My roommate accidentally drank a Diet Mountain Dew the other day and had to sleep it off.

I know exactly how he feels.

Everyone can tell how you feel all the time because they can look at your face.

You have to be honest with yourself.

I just wish I knew how.

I'm considering using 'Ferrari' as an adjective more often. Like, it would be totally Ferrari if I ever saw my dad cry.

You Are So Pensive

I worry you are going to crack like an egg that I've never heard of.

I wouldn't know how to clean you up.

I want to put you out but you aren't such a fire to me anymore.

I remember you.

I have told you I love you with varying degrees of conviction at least 1,400 times.

We have had sex until we couldn't or it hurt and until it couldn't hurt any longer and both agreed that we fit nicely together.

Sometimes it's not enough to fit with someone.

Most people fit.

I am trying so hard to fit in at least 47% of the time.

You are trying so hard to let me go.

It's enough.

There's something you should know about me. When I was nine years old I became the youngest father of all time and incidentally the coolest boy of all time for exactly 14 minutes until some kid in Florida managed to swing all the way over the top of the swing set. He was only the coolest boy on the planet for a split second before his heart exploded in his chest and his stomach got stuck in his throat, but his memory will live on. Meanwhile, I have this rude teenage son who is basically my age, calls me his 'roommate' and won't listen to a word I say.

If you would feel sorry for me right away that would be great, I could just take that right to the bank.

No one has ever gotten more people to feel sorry for them than Kurt Cobain except for Anne Frank.

No one has ever gotten more people to feel sorry for them than Anne Frank except for Jesus. No one has ever made more money than Jesus except me.

I am making so much money when I move through this world, flowing through the spaces in each moment that passes through me.

An ape does exactly what I do at the zoo when I sit on my stoop in the summer time.

So do you when you watch me out of the corner of your eye.

You don't have to shave anything for me. It just doesn't matter. You're just a ball of fuzz to me anyway. I want to keep you that way. I'd even cover you in furs. Girl, you know I'd kill a man for you but I wouldn't touch a dolphin, no no. You can be so furry to me all the time. Baby baby baby you are the youngest person I have ever met and when I squeeze the sides of your skull we are both screaming at each other in our own language and I wouldn't expect anyone else to understand.

Would you wear that clickety clack plastic shit in your hair for me if I braided it?

The Night Ministry Van Comes by the Library and
Gives Free Hot Dogs to All the Homeless People Who
Hang Out Around There at Night

They usually stay all day until the hot dog van comes back again. My friend got one from them one time but I didn't. I felt weird about it because I live in an apartment with my own hot dogs.

The homeless people have started hanging out inside the library during the day too. In the afternoon, the kids from the grade schools in the neighborhood all go to the library and use the public computers and play their *Dora the Explorer* video games. The homeless guys mostly watch YouTube and porn. There aren't as many homeless women, but I think I saw one of them watching a Celine Dion video.

The library only has one security guard. He's an old black guy who's been working there forever. He wears a jacket that's way too big for him, the sleeves go over his hands, and he transfers his weight from side to side when he walks like he has trouble bending his knees or doesn't actually have them. He travels slowly around the library in a big predictable loop. When he passes by, the homeless guys just change tabs to something that isn't porn then switch back once he's gone.

The water faucet in my bathroom only makes hot water. I try to wash my hands before it gets too hot but there is a moment at the end where I usually feel intense discomfort from the heat for a second before pulling away.

A lot of people have been burned alive by scalding hot water.

A lot of people are being permanently bullied by their own nervous systems.

A lot of people have probably tried to summon the devil so they could sell their souls and were disappointed when nothing happened.

The Dalai Lama says we need to find ways to incorporate teaching warm-heartedness in our education system.

I would imagine he is probably the most qualified person to be burned alive but I hope that doesn't happen.

Favorite Flavors:

Heat

Dirt

Income

Porcelain

Tank

Water (not flavorless)

Tear

Bark

Humidity

Drug snot

Toothpick

Turn-ons Include:

Ball pits

Rotisseries

'Hot' peas

Hair/Fur

Groans

Cat posture

What I think Israeli dance clubs are like

Phones

Men/Women (Adults)

Databases

Chill parents

Telling people that I thought David Byrne was Robin Williams as a kid listening to "Once in a Lifetime"

Small business owners

Kindly worded copywriting in bank advertisements

When people use the phrase 'bread and circuses' smugly

Lake Michigan in August

• A snowdrift

• A deer running somewhere (quietly)

• Someone smiling at me and I know why and it's a good thing about myself

• Smelling gasoline in a parking garage

• Imagining Mozart saying something racist (would give me a lot of pleasure, maybe not beautiful but pretty funny)

• People having unrelated arguments about race/politics/gender in the comment section of a nice song

• A train car of 100 commuters returning from the city to the suburbs (silently)

• Someone jogging and looking really upset about it

• An animated snowdrift

• Someone really cool wearing a gold chain and twerking until they fly the flag at half mast or the economy recovers (whichever comes first)

• Being broken up with via silent treatment and just figuring it out eventually

• Saying really mean things that you don't mean to get a reaction and regretting them but not bothering to apologize because you were ignored

• Thinking about mirroring people facial movements and cadence patterns while speaking to them in order to create a rapport as opposed to just being yourself because you're sure that won't work

• Your family being disappointed in your life decisions but still forwarding you humorous emails with pictures of animals and children

• The bus picks you up right outside of your house

• Not knowing how you cat ever feels really

They were wearing matching *Looney Tunes* t-shirts, the kind where the characters wear backward hats and display an aggressive, confrontational attitude.

They had been sharing an elephant ear (fried sugar bread snack) but didn't finish it. I saw two female lions chase down a baby zebra and rip its striped skin off its body in front of its whole family while a male lion sat under a tree and watched and yawned.

I saw myself grow older over time.

I watched myself dissolve, becoming permanently incorporated into something else, forgetting what I was, with these brand new cells.

I want to go to where God works and smack the dick out of his mouth.

You fucked up on 'time,' bro. And I know you still fuck with the devil.

I'm not supposed to be writing poetry right now. I'm supposed to be doing something else but I don't know how to do anything else.

There are two Batman themed roller coasters at Six Flags but Batman doesn't care about you and neither do I.

Sometimes people do things on purpose to make you upset and then feel victimized when you get upset with them.

When my brother was first born, I was told I walked up to my mom and said, "Congratulations," and the nurses laughed because they thought it was cute and I thought they were making fun of me and got angry.

I used to make my hand into a claw-shape and shake it in my little brother's face and make a noise like 'nn-nn-nn-nnnn.' Not sure how he felt about that. Probably bad.

Paul Hanson Clark ended one of his poems with a line that read, "There are innocent people on death row," and that is how I will end this too.

Why 'Matt Damon' and I Are No Longer on Speaking Terms

14 Oct 2013

'Amanda Bynes' and I first meet on the Internet.

She's 20/f/in. I'm 26/m/il.

'Amanda Bynes' likes a story I wrote about accidentally drinking too much cough syrup and going to the mall.

It's 2 p.m. on a Wednesday afternoon and I'm drinking whiskey in the kitchen with my roommate and next-door neighbor when 'Amanda Bynes' requests to video chat.

I accept and she sends me a link to what she calls her 'nude blog.'

I ask if it's ok the show my friends and she gladly gives permission.

Everyone approves of the blog and we all agree that 'Amanda Bynes' seems pretty cool before packing up our liquor in a tote bag and heading to the park to fly kites.

It's summertime and I just don't give a shit.

'Amanda Bynes' asks me for my number and I give it to her. We text each other a lot over the following week.

I like texting 'Amanda Bynes.'

She's playful and I'm curious about her. She seems to think everything I say is funny. Her sense of humor is pretty vulgar but she seems like a sweet person.

She doesn't seem dumb.

I'm drunk again, this time on the front stoop at night with friends, sending her a series of messages bragging about an 'iced-out Livestrong bracelet' that I don't have.

Now she wants to drive from Indiana to see me.

I agree and three hours later 'Amanda Bynes' arrives in a red coupe with a trash-littered floor and a sticker that reads 'Take Yo Panties Off' on the windshield.

She's all smiles and they're all good.

They make me do the same. We bounce off each other all night.

'Amanda Bynes' ends up staying for three days. When it's time for her to leave, I don't want her to go. She says I should come back with her to Indiana where she shares an apartment with her ex-boyfriend until the lease ends in a month. It's possible. I only work three days a week and have the next four days off.

"Is he going to be cool?" I ask.

"Yeah, of course. 'Matt Damon' is really chill. He's really busy with work most of the time anyway."

I'm skeptical.

"He's had girls spend the night before and it was fine. If I have someone over he's not going to bother me."

I agree. 'Amanda Bynes' and I listen to trap music and chain smoke in between tollbooth stops. We pass a black-and-white sign on the side of the road that reads 'Hell Is Real.' I take a picture and we laugh and laugh.

Then it's silent. Neither of us speaks for a bit.

We exchange glances, seeking assurance that it's ok to be quiet. Trap beats vibrate the speaker and rattle the trunk. We share the stillness through Indiana.

On arrival, I'm surprised 'Amanda Bynes' lives in an actual house rather than an apartment. She parks in the garage out back next to the shell of a hollowed out vehicle. There's a mattress covered in mysterious stains propped against the wall but I don't want to solve the mystery very badly.

'Matt Damon' works on cars for a living, 'Amanda' explains, gesturing at the shell. He's 28, she tells me. I didn't ask.

'Amanda Bynes' invites me inside and shows me around. All of her things are in boxes in her room. The bedroom floor is covered in magazine cutouts. There's the disembodied head of a muscular black man along with a speech bubble that reads 'are you ok?' They're for a project she's working on, she says. It's not finished.

'Matt Damon' comes home early. He is super chill, as promised. Possibly too chill. He walks right up to me and shakes my hand. Firm.

"You're that writer from the Internet, right?" he asks.

"Yeah," I reply.

"'Amanda' made me read that one story, the one about you getting high on cough syrup at the mall. Funny stuff, man."

"Thanks."

"Did you really do that?"

"Yeah."

"Haha. Wildness. That's cool though. I used to robotrip in junior high when I couldn't find weed."

"I was just really sick and drank too much on accident."

"Oh. Haha. How?"

"I was chasing NyQuil with it and I guess I wasn't paying very close attention."

"Huh. Well, I guess that's pretty funny too. Ha. Yeah. Oh man. You must have been surprised as shit."

"Yeah. Didn't see that coming."

"Oh man. I know. Totally."

This is going better than expected. 'Amanda Bynes' is in the other room playing with her pet rats through the bars of their cage.

'Matt Damon' announces he is going to bake some chicken nuggets and offers me some. I politely decline and he smiles at me for what feels like a long time. He reaches into the freezer and produces an economy-size bag of nuggets without breaking eye contact.

I ask 'Amanda Bynes' if we can go hang out somewhere else for a while and she cheerfully agrees. She says goodbye to the rats in a baby voice and we pass through the kitchen on our way out.

"Hey, you guys," 'Matt Damon' shouts after us.

"Have a great time tonight, alright? Be safe."

I assure 'Matt Damon' that we will and he waves goodbye, whistling what I believe is the Andy Griffith Show theme song while greasing up a pan with a stick of butter.

"I'm probably going to die tonight," I think to myself.

'Amanda Bynes' slams the screen door shut.

"Bye, little shit baby," she shouts back into the house. She grins at me.

I could die tonight, yeah.

I'm thinking we'll just see how this plays out.

Later that evening, 'Amanda Bynes' and I are sitting on her floor admiring her collages. There's a cutout of a malamute and a speech bubble that reads "chillin wit dogs." I can hear 'Matt Damon' moving things around in his bedroom. I ask if it's ok if we close the door and 'Amanda Bynes' says sure. She shuts it and I take my pants off immediately. I ask if it's ok if we lock it too and she says that she would but it doesn't have a lock.

I'm considering putting my pants back on when 'Matt Damon' enters the room with his laptop and a big old smile. He wants to show us a youtube video he's got all loaded up. In it, the singer performs a song about how he can't measure up to the ex-boyfriend of the girl he recently started seeing. It's supposed to be funny.

'Matt Damon' sets the laptop on the floor on top of the magazine cutouts and presses play. 'Amanda Bynes' is laughing throughout and 'Matt Damon' keeps looking over at me and laughing in my direction even harder during the parts that seem like they'd be the funniest. Hahahaha. Haha. Yeah. I don't think it's funny.

'Amanda Bynes' thanks 'Matt Damon' for sharing but I'm not so grateful. Once he leaves, I ask if it's ok if he doesn't hang out with us anymore tonight. She says she's sorry; he just gets excited about videos and probably won't be back.

'Matt Damon' returns ten minutes later. He's holding a pair of yellow basketball shorts.

"Heard you didn't have any pants," he says with a smile and tosses them at me.

I say thanks. No problem, he says. 'Matt Damon' asks me if I like acid. I look to 'Amanda Bynes' and she nods vigorously. I say yes and he goes into his room and brings back a plastic sandwich bag containing a sheet with various Peanuts characters on it. He hands me two Snoopy tabs and tells me they're 'on the house.' His house. Because this is his house, he says. 'Amanda Bynes' laughs at that one. Not funny.

I thank 'Matt Damon' for letting me spend my vacation in his house. He says I'm totally welcome and asks 'Amanda Bynes' if he may speak with her for a minute and they step outside. I put on the shorts and think I'm probably not going to take this Snoopy acid but put it in my wallet anyway.

'Amanda Bynes' returns 10 minutes later and apologizes, saying everything is fine now. I ask her what is going on and she reassures me it's fine now. We won't be bothered again.

'Matt Damon' returns fifteen minutes later. He's holding construction paper and a handful of sharpies. He says he noticed the cutouts on the floors and was wondering if we wanted to do some arts and crafts with him.

"Fuck yeah," 'Amanda Bynes' shouts and grabs some paper. I reluctantly take a glue stick and a sharpie from a beaming 'Matt Damon.' It's almost 3 in the morning. We get right to work.

I'm absent-mindedly gluing some of magazine cutouts onto construction paper while 'Matt Damon' carefully cuts little shapes in his construction paper. He's looking over at me periodically. I don't look back but can see in my peripheral that he isn't smiling anymore.

'Matt Damon' mentions offhand that, while he did have a girl over to spend the night once, they didn't have sex because the walls here are paper-thin and that would be really uncool. I nod and glue a cutout of a model's head onto an SUV.

We all finish our crafts and present them to each other. 'Matt Damon' declares that 'Amanda Bynes'' is the best before announcing that he's going to play video games. As soon as he leaves, 'Amanda Bynes' and I hop into bed. I really don't want to have sex here. She gets right on top of me and starts grinding away in vain on the softest possible dick.

"I am going to die tonight," I think to myself.

The TV 'Matt Damon' is playing on is adjacent to the wall next to the bed we're lying in. He's in there pretending to shoot aliens and the sound of gunfire and explosions is creating an effect similar to what feels like a pretty decent war zone.

'Amanda Bynes' says I should just relax and that 'Matt

Damon' won't hear us. The game is so loud, he can't hear us. She takes off my shirt. She grinds some more and the bed squeaks like a cartoon.

The volume of the gunfire increases.

'Amanda Bynes' grinds.

Squeak. Squeak. Squeak. The gunfire stops. A brief ceasefire. I'm next.

We are both about halfway undressed when 'Matt Damon' bursts into the room pointing at me and shouting. 'Amanda Bynes' whirls around and positions herself in between us, naked, guarding over me like a mother lion.

'Matt Damon' is taken aback. Nonetheless, he presents his argument: what we're doing isn't cool. Therefore I must leave immediately. It's after 3 a.m. and I'm hundreds of miles from home.

This doesn't appear to be going as 'Matt Damon' planned. He is breathing heavily. His face is red; his eyes are watery. 'Amanda Bynes' won't budge. Her glare is fierce and I'm her cub.

'Matt Damon' looks hurt. He asks 'Amanda Bynes' if I took that acid he gave me. Apparently he and I are no longer on speaking terms. She tells him I did but that's not true. She's lying so he won't start a fight out of respect for the assumed fact that I'm on drugs. After some debate, he convinces her to leave the room so he may speak with me alone. I sit up and he takes a seat next to me on the bed.

'Matt Damon' somberly presents the facts: he welcomed me into his home and I violated his trust. I'm still wearing his basketball shorts even. The nerve of me. I feel kind of guilty but not really and then I don't feel guilty at all because fuck 'Matt Damon.'

I prepare all of the knowledge I can remember from grade school karate lessons but what I tell him is that I was just a bit confused because he had treated me so nicely today. He smiles and shrugs.

"Well, yeah."

And that was that. 'Amanda Bynes' and I leave without incident. She spends the next half hour apologizing. She says she'll take me home if I want her to but I don't want to make her travel that far this late.

We decide to take a few of her Adderall and go to a park where we swing on the swings and chain smoke until sun up. She's quiet and I don't need to look to her for assurance to see if it's ok. She seems like she wants to cry and I expect her to. Instead she tells me that she's glad I came. I tell her I am too. And it's true.

She smiles at me and it's a good one.

It makes me do the same.

I
Do
It.

15 Nov 2013

A man named Rudy Eugene ate a homeless person's face underneath a highway last summer.

The police claimed Rudy was on a drug called 'bath salts.'

They said the drugs drove Rudy crazy and compelled him to tear the man's flesh off with his teeth.

The news called him the 'Miami Bath Salts Cannibal.'

But Rudy Eugene wasn't on bath salts.

I Forgive You in the Forest

With the woods and the trees.

It takes a lot out of me.

I rub a leaf on my sweaty forehead.

"We should be very sympathetic to teenagers because they are just starting to realize how terrible everything is and if I remember correctly it is very painful," I say at your face.

"I want to be downsized from my middle management job at a reputable company during a thunderstorm in 20 years," is the sort of noise you make in my direction.

"I am insanely jealous of you, like so super jealous," we say at each other at the same time and it's true.

And things orbit around.

Continents move.

Radioactive materials decay.

When people are heavy, sit with them. When entropy increases, order me around.

Tax my energy over time like everything else.

I will chaperone you to a relevant outdoor music festival and you can push me around in a bassinet once we get there.

Shoot me with a gun in the United States of America.

I am going to put on a pair of white jeans and you are going to push me down the stairs.

I am going to put on a pair of black jeans and you are going to roll over my toes with your car on accident.

I am going to put on a pair of blue jeans and you are going to sell my organs on the black market to pay off your student loans.

I am going to put on a pair of yellow jeans and you are going to put my other jeans in the dryer so that they are all toasty warm and then watch me try each of them on one at a time.

I am going to put on a pair of green jeans and you are going to show me a power point presentation on the dangers of sexting.

I am going to put on a pair of purple jeans and you are going to drive me out to the arboretum and we are going to go for a hike and not really talk to each other that much and wonder if its a problem.

I am going to put on a pair of oversized jean shorts and you are going to take me to the pet store and we are going to look at the different puppies and consider playing with some of them but decide not to and go to a restaurant instead.

I am going to put on a pair of knee high cut off shorts and you are going to ask me about a bunch of Cool

Bands I have never heard of while we are riding bikes. You are going to shout unfamiliar names back at me while we are riding on the street and I am going to pretend I understand by smiling and shouting Yeah but I can 't really hear you because it's too windy.

I am going to put on a pair of pleated department store khaki slacks and you are going to drive me to the mall and pretend to be interested in buying a cellphone case from an overzealous salesman at a kiosk because you are lonely even though we are together.

I am going to put on a pair of stiff corduroys and you are going to lower the basketball hoop on my parents driveway to six feet so we can both do slam dunks.

I am going to put on a pair of long johns and you are going to try to get me into a critically acclaimed cable TV series on Netflix and I am going to do my best to feign interest.

I am going to put on a pair of sweatpants and wander out into the forest in the middle of the night, in the dead of winter, with my iPod playing static on repeat, and you are going to remember me the way I wanted to be remembered; by my collective social media output.

We Melt

When you scraped off your semi permanent gel nail polish at McDonald's.

While I was trying in vain to download *Mulan* with their free Wi-Fi.

It started raining and you said your stomach hurt.

The movie was at 6 percent and there were 5 minutes left before close.

That big lady was standing by the door staring us down because she wanted us to leave.

And it was raining harder.

And you smiled at me.

And left the nail polish chrysalis on the table.

I melted and it wasn't our problem.

We melt together all the time.

These days.

In all sorts of ways.

I promised I wouldn't say that you are better than me anymore.

So I won't.

I'm an American and my truck was built by God.

A drunk guy with long, greasy hair approached me aggressively.

He "stepped" to me.

He stood close as if I was supposed to do something next, so I stared at him.

We stared into each other's eyes for a little bit.

His face was covered in sores and he seemed more frightened than anything.

Something was going on with him and I could see whatever it was overflowing.

"What happened," I asked.

He paused for a moment.

Then he told me I looked like Jesus.

I laughed and worried that he might think I was laughing at him.

"What happened to the world?" he asked.

I said I wasn't sure.

He told me, "You drink, you fuck your life up," and walked over to an old man who was also waiting for the bus.

The old man gave him a cigarette, which he smoked while we boarded the bus and rode away.

I Am Mad at the Ocean

I resent its relentless force.

I am kicking the water and punching the waves.

Feel less guilty.

Did my part.

I get mad at the beach.

I kick sand at a palm tree or whatever they're called.

I see a couple laying out and sigh and throw my shoes into the sea.

When I was a teenage referee of tween soccer games the tweens used to say a lot of one-liners.

For instance, they'd steal the ball and say "I'll Take That."

When I was a teenage referee of tween baseball games I once called a tween out at first base and his mom got mad.

She ran up to the chain linked face and screamed at me and called me a 'faggot.'

Everyone wants you to change.

Everyone is controlling.

It's fine.

Every night I die in my dreams.

Every morning I am reborn.

It's exhausting.

We Are Otters Now

I could tell you were excited.

I could see it in your eyelids.

You show yourself off.

Give yourself up.

And away.

Now you are still here.

We are otters.

Floating down the river in your bed.

Hand held like paws.

So we don't float apart.

People are being born and dying.

Ripping each other off and to shreds.

Loving each other to pieces and to death.

We don't care.

We are otters now.

At the rate I'm going, I will surely become a dad.

Not bragging, it's just a simple fact of life.

Getting alarmingly close to fatherhood.

I want my Future Son to be a kind man.

The kind of man that cares about how animals feel.

Baby boy.

I am going to fill up your bathtub with cake mix and then give you all the hot water you need 2 succeed.

The fight or flight impulse that got us here is now making us sick and crazy.

When there is nowhere to fly and fighting isn't reasonable.

As in the case of sending or receiving a Big Email.

That adrenaline just goes into your body.

It works its way through you.

Today I am thinking about how to listen to my body.

I want my son to be a sensitive lover.

Want to step in and show him 'how to swing' but am not sure what I mean by that exactly.

Baby boy.

You are better than the others.

A crescendo of feeling will often befall your ass because you are my bb.

Just ignore it.

And keep playing the guitar.

Dad jeans.
Cargo shorts.
Plaid cargo
shorts. We
got 'em all.
Come by my
house I'll sell
you my dad's
pants while
he's at work
who cares.

Put it on your shelf and when you feel that way again, we can both look at it together and laugh.

Guilt is a useless emotion and you can feed me through a straw if you want.

You can shave my neck tonight; I can't see it in the mirror.

Vietnam is a dope word and I hope you become a mom or dad at exactly the moment that you want to be one.

I want to write a story where everyone is a good person and is nice to each other but they die at the end and my mom reads it and says its nice but why did they have to die at the end.

I want to live a life where I am not so much achieving goals and having success but scratching out dull urges like little itches as quickly as they come and I can't control it and don't want to.

Everything takes forever and I think that's great.

I want to take forever too.

I was pushing my son on a riverside swing.

Pushed too hard, he flew off and landed on a crocodiles back in the river.

It was real chill about it but it still ate my damn son.

Things have gotten harder for me since.

The only place I can relax and be myself these days is parked in bank parking lots after dark.

I just like knowing the money is safe inside.

"Maybe you are never too old to join a gang," I tell myself as I drive through the only Subway drive-thru in the world.

I'm being so selfish I cannot even appreciate this rare drive-thru.

Yesterday I jogged through a snow storm and was un-aware of how beautiful it was because I was too busy thinking about myself.

"Start your own tribe," I was thinking.

"I am always starting over," I thought.

Once, when I was a child, a dog chased my dad up a tree.

Mom brought home a new dad eventually but sometimes I wonder if Old Dad is still up there.

Things have been getting better lately.

I met a woman who makes slightly less money than me.

Together, we watch shows.

We are both explaining the plot to this Rom-com to each other at the same time so loudly that we can't hear or concentrate on the film.

Tonight, I am a cop.

So are you.

We put each other under arrest and sit in the back seat of the cruiser waiting for someone to drive us home.

When you are kissing me I feel like you are holding my head in the sink underneath the faucet.

A French-kiss water board.

I can't even feel your tongue, it's mostly water.

Love is function of dedication.

You are the end and I give up.

Go ahead and put your fist inside me and make me say things that, while amusing, may not necessarily be in my best interest.

"Romantic love is a trap designed to expand capitalism," I recite on my way to work.

"This world is a slow beast," you mutter at your desk.

♪ ♫ <(.__.)> ♫ ♪ <(.__.)> ♪ ♫

(.__) . *!*!*!* (.__.)

(.__) .<(.__.)

♪ (.__)> .<(.__.) ♪

♪ ♫ ♪ ♫ <(.__.)> <(.__.)> ♪ ♫ ♪ ♫

Sometimes I think that maybe one day we humans will build our own sun and live forever.

Then I do the dishes.

I deleted my Facebook.

I reactivated my Facebook.

   The San Andreas Fault didn't move.

I deleted my Facebook.

I reactivated my Facebook.

   The icecaps just sat there.

And ~140 million people kept having variously satis-
fying degrees of sex and I sat here fading into a cool
blue haze.

It's blue to me because that's the color I see when I
close my eyes in a dimly lit room and that is what I'm
doing right now.

If I can't see you, you cant see me.

And if I tell you I have been a genius before you'll just have to take my word for it. Because everything is just so dumb right now.

With the ocean and the noise

And the things I can't see and don't want to.

You can relate to that right?

You can relate to being dumb under the summer sun in my line of sight.

Perhaps you feel bad in a lot of ways you just aren't aware of right now.

Maybe I care for you more than myself sometimes.

That is an example of one of the things you may feel bad about.

Sorry to make you aware of it.

If we were standing at the top of a tall building I would tell you I am afraid of heights.

If we were at your mom's house I would tell you I am afraid of your mom.

If we were on drugs I would tell you I am afraid of 'on drugs' and that maybe if we worry about the future enough together maybe we can stop it from coming.

Give me a mole test: a pop mole quiz.

Do not give me time to prepare, just touch me on different parts of my body and ask me if I have a mole there or not.

Chances are I wont know where most of my own moles are.

Sit hard on my face until it becomes a shiny little diamond.

Kiss me tongue-wise on my slippery mineral lips.

You are making a profit.

I lose myself and find myself in you all the time and if you would like to be further disappointed I will link you to an article that shows that 1/4 of the species on earth are beetles.

I come in waves.

I'm sorry but I am like the waves.

Catch me when I'm cresting and just leave me at the beach.

I'll be there when you get back.

I have
a lot of
thoughts
I'm not
sharing
with you.

I will go hard for you in the mountains.

At the mall.

On the beach.

And in your dreams.

I will watch *Jurassic Park 3D* with you even though I've already seen it in 'Regular D.'

I will watch *Jurassic Park 2* with you in 2D now.

And in 3D when it comes out.

I will watch *Jurassic Park 3 3D* with you too, I guess.

Dimensions have little to no effect on how hard I am willing to go for you.

I ask my co-worker, "Ballin' hard or hardly ballin'?"

He gets so into it.

Truth be told, I love motherfuckers when they haul ass.

It's a love thang.

Just drop the whitest milk.

The tightest milk.

I drive my car all night and it feels so right.

Finally, a car for me.

Martin Luther King had a car.

I am a car.

2 fast.

2 scared.

4 ever.

Goodbye Kauai

The sun sits on top of you in Kauai.

Every day feels the same.

I rubbed coconut oil from a brown bottle on my skin because I felt like I might as well.

Every day we pick the little shy weeds that curl up when you touch them, on Andre's farm.

One woman with miles and miles of the Planet Earth, trees that make fruit, and her own waterfall, with money she was given, and so much religion to share. Everyone agrees with Andre.

Everyone works for Andre.

Raymond works for Andre and he's my favorite.

In his 40s, he looks much younger.

A Canadian with a surfer's lilt, he lived in China for 8 years and claims to speak fluent Cantonese.

I'll take his word for it.

Evelyn and I go out to dinner with him and he orders a whole roast duck in Cantonese.

The waiter says he can't understand him.

Raymond says he was just indignant that a white man was speaking the language so well.

I'll take his word for it.

I'm all oiled up and the sun is hot and low in the sky when Mark drives up the road to Raymond's shed.

He gets out of his truck, goes in the door, and comes out with a chainsaw.

"Fuck no," Raymond shouts and runs to climb over the fence, sprinting out onto the dirt road to block Mark's truck.

Mark gets out and starts beating Raymond with his whole fist, in the chest, and then in the back once Raymond folds.

Evelyn drops what she's doing and runs after them, shouting.

I stand and watch.

Raymond is crying.

Mark looks shaken.

"You're not a dread, bro," Raymond sniffles.

"Dreads don't hit people."

Last week, I was smoking weed with Raymond in his shed.

There is no electricity in here, just a 12-piece drum set he played for me once.

It is very dark and Raymond is still and quiet at the end of the day.

After moving so fast and so much, he is now a stoned

shadow in a corner.

He gestures at the chainsaw.

"If things ever get bad enough, I'm just going to take that thing and end it."

I laugh like a monkey.

Tomorrow is 85 degrees and sunny and Raymond is up earlier than we are, banging on our window, asking if he can cut up avocados and bananas in our blender.

This place is full of people who thought things would be different here.

They were wrong.

It's more the same than it's ever been, and there's just so much more of you to fill your days.

Recently, I've been wearing these all-weather sandals every day since I found them in storage.

I bought them when we moved to Hawaii together.

I'm sorry that you are such an idiot.

You explained to me that no one can 'know' whether or not crystals have healing properties.

This turned into a fight somehow.

You liked to tell me 'everything's relative.'

I guess we are related too and when I fuck you like a psycho it is probably even more of a sin against nature.

I'd like to French exhale into you like you're a two liter

bottle of Mountain Dew.

I want to construct a ship inside of you and we can sail off the edge of this flat Earth.

We almost made it.

Again & Again

you & i

we will see each other

again
 & again
   & again

until we have been each other

over
 & over
   & it is very exciting to die

this way with you
 all of the time

yes, i am certain you have lived my own life at least
400 thousand times

yes, it sounds very boring but i'm glad
it's always different

when i am in love
the moon is the same as it ever was
but not to me

i'm glad it's always different

so i will tell you now
that before i had only been myself
alone, with something too heavy to share

now i'm with me when i'm right here
in so much of you, us
with so much of one
another, together
recurring, forever

don't you wish you did things differently?
don't wish you did things differently

returns are eternal

& you're always right here now
  & you've always come back before

again
& again
  & again
    & again
      & again

with us in so much of one
another, together

i know i said your skin is a wave
i'm sorry it's so simple
but nothing else has ever really happened
this is the only thing that has ever happened

your breath & mine combined
so much, all the time

& i taste like so much of me to you
  & you taste just like you always have
    & it's always the same
      & and it's always changed
        & all this, this is all that

remains

Heiko Julien (b. 1986) lives in Chicago.

CPSIA information can be obtained
at www.ICGtesting.com
Printed in the USA
BVOW06s2128181216

470772BV00008B/76/P